What
Is
Death?

$\mathcal{V}_{L}\mathcal{B}$ *Veronica Lane Books*

What Is Death?

By Etan Boritzer   Illustrated by Nancy Forrest

 Veronica Lane Books

513 Wilshire Blvd #282, Santa Monica, CA 90401, USA (800) 651.1001

Library of Congress Cataloging-In-Publication Data
        Boritzer, Etan, 1950-
        What Is Death?

Library of Congress Catalog Card Number 98-075397

Summary: The author presents the concept of death to children with examples of customs and beliefs from various religions and cultures.

ISBN 0-9637597-4-4 (bound)   ISBN 0-9637597-5-2 (pbk.)

1. Death - Comparative studies - Juvenile Literature 155.937
    I.Forrest, Nancy, 1951-   I.Title

Dedicated to the memory of George.

. . . to the children

of the world . . .

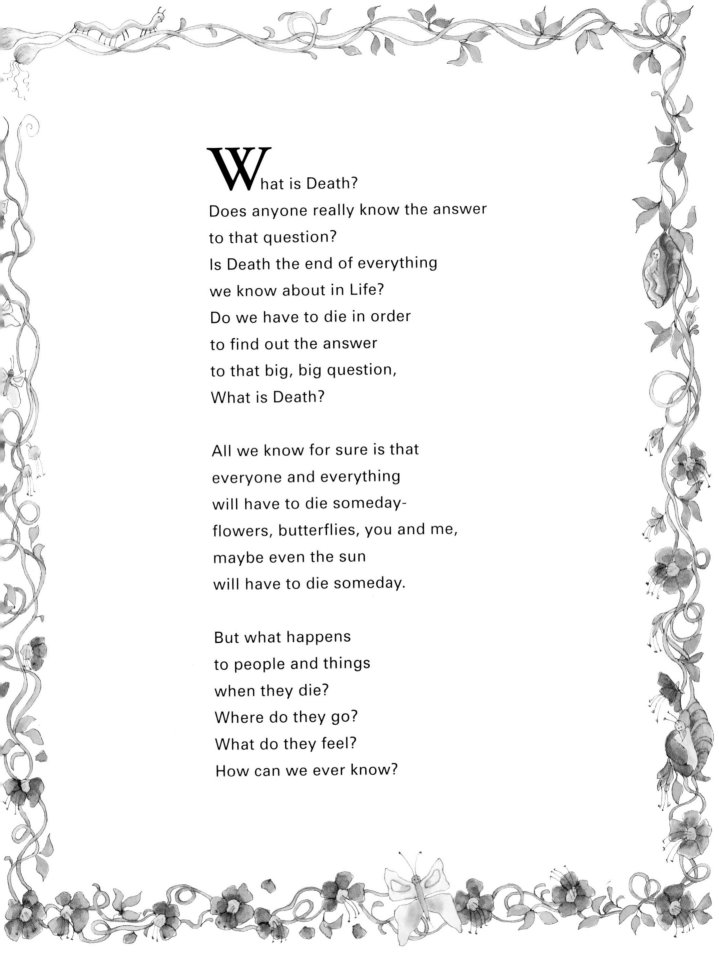

What is Death?
Does anyone really know the answer
to that question?
Is Death the end of everything
we know about in Life?
Do we have to die in order
to find out the answer
to that big, big question,
What is Death?

All we know for sure is that
everyone and everything
will have to die someday-
flowers, butterflies, you and me,
maybe even the sun
will have to die someday.

But what happens
to people and things
when they die?
Where do they go?
What do they feel?
How can we ever know?

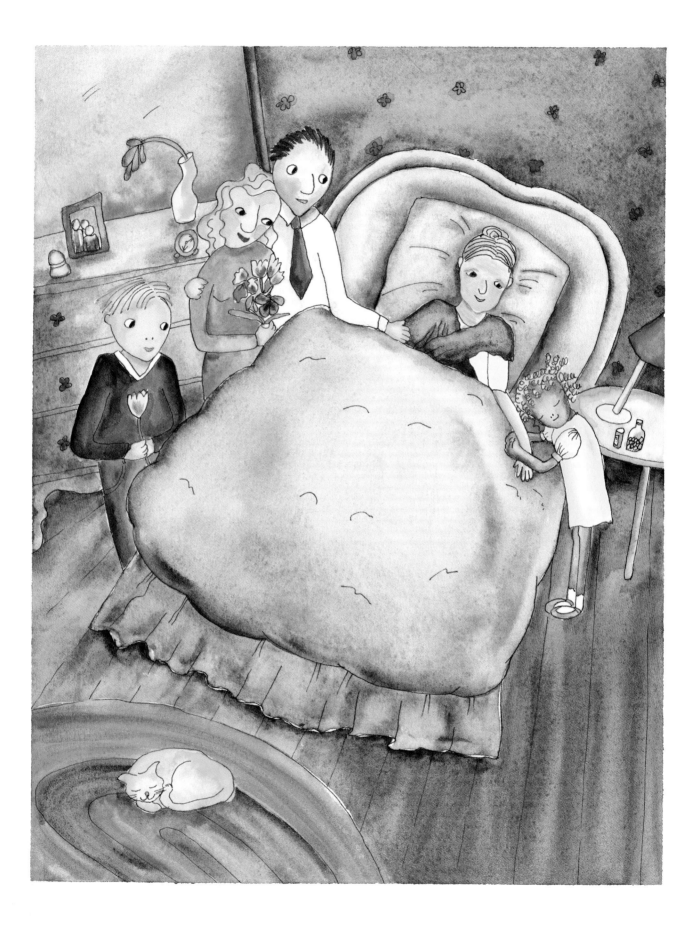

We know that when a person's
heart stops beating,
he or she dies.

The heart can stop beating
if a person gets very old
or very sick
or if an accident happens.
(An accident is when someone
gets hurt by surprise.)

Sometimes Death
is a quiet and peaceful thing,
but sometimes it is not.

Death happens every day
but it is one of Life's deepest mysteries.
(A mystery is like a puzzle
whose answer is hidden from us.)

But *why* does everyone want to know
about the mystery of Death?

Have you ever gone into a dark room
where you couldn't see anything?
Maybe you were scared
until you turned on the light.
Maybe people ask What is Death?
because they are scared of Death.

Have you ever walked along the beach
and seen a dead fluffy white seagull
lying in the sand?
Maybe people ask What is Death?
because they want to know
why beautiful things die.

Have you ever had a friend
or someone you love die?
Maybe people ask What is Death?
because they get really sad
and miss the person they love
if that person dies.

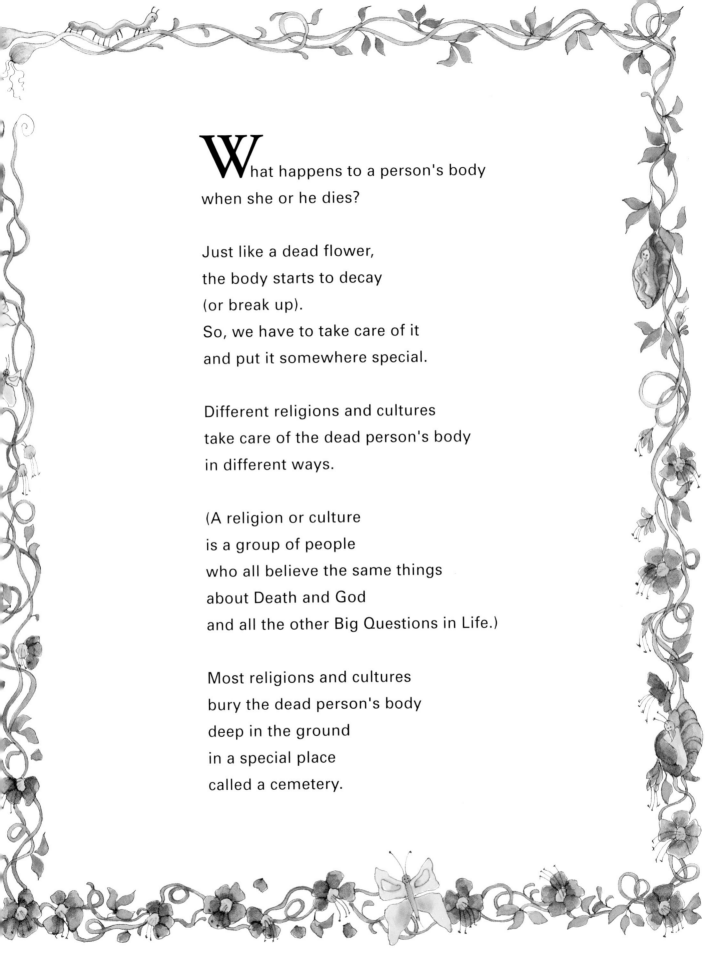

What happens to a person's body
when she or he dies?

Just like a dead flower,
the body starts to decay
(or break up).
So, we have to take care of it
and put it somewhere special.

Different religions and cultures
take care of the dead person's body
in different ways.

(A religion or culture
is a group of people
who all believe the same things
about Death and God
and all the other Big Questions in Life.)

Most religions and cultures
bury the dead person's body
deep in the ground
in a special place
called a cemetery.

Some religions and cultures
put the dead person's body in the ocean.

Other religions and cultures
turn the dead person's body
into ashes and put the ashes
in a special place.

Some cultures and religions long ago
put the dead body in a big clay jar
and buried it underground.

Also a long time ago
the Egyptians wrapped dead people
in white cloth and buried them,
along with lots of gold and jewels,
deep inside big pyramids in the desert.

Maybe you have a friend
who had someone he or she loved die.

Maybe your friend had a Grandpa,
whom he really loved
and who really loved him.
And maybe his Grandpa told your friend
funny stories that made him laugh,
and gave him presents,
and made him feel good.

Maybe his Grandpa got old or sick
and one day he died.
And maybe after he died,
your friend's Grandpa looked like
he was just sleeping.
But your friend knew
that his Grandpa couldn't wake up,
and your friend felt really sad.

Where did all his Grandpa's
funny stories go?
Where did all the
wonderful inside stuff and all the love
that his Grandpa had for your friend go,
if his body was just lying there,
looking like he was taking a nap?

Where does all the inside stuff,
like feelings, thoughts, ideas, and love,
go if a person's heart stops beating
and his body dies?

Sure, we use our bodies
to get around every day-
to go to school, to eat,
to play, to sleep, to live.
But what about all the inside stuff?

We know there are many ways
to put away a dead person's body,
but if your friend's Grandpa was buried,
did all his love get buried too?
What happens to all the inside stuff
when a person dies?

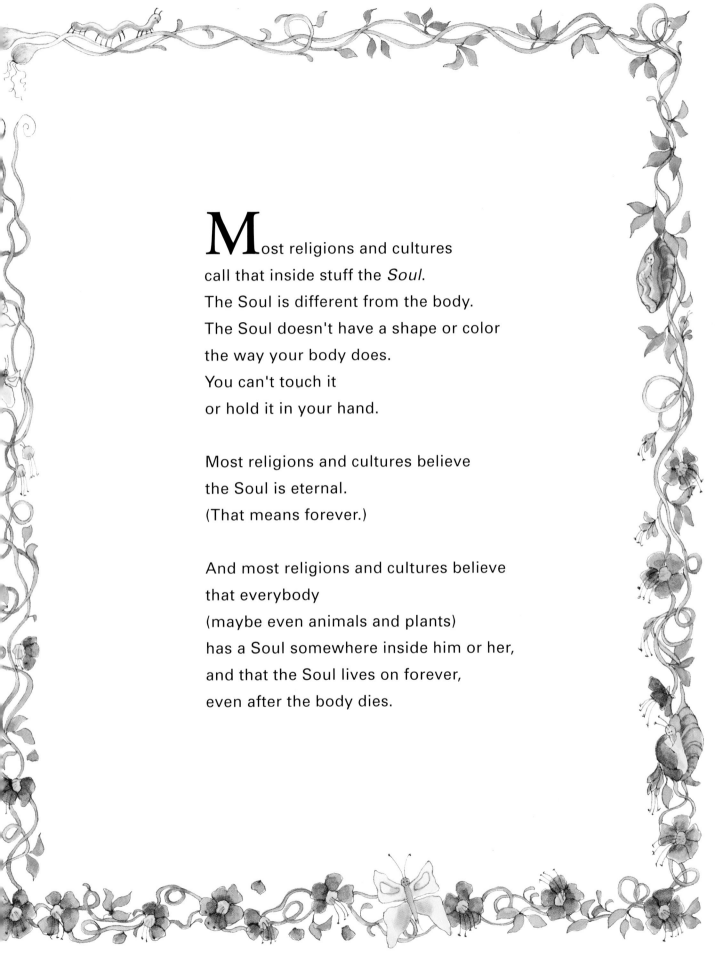

Most religions and cultures
call that inside stuff the *Soul*.
The Soul is different from the body.
The Soul doesn't have a shape or color
the way your body does.
You can't touch it
or hold it in your hand.

Most religions and cultures believe
the Soul is eternal.
(That means forever.)

And most religions and cultures believe
that everybody
(maybe even animals and plants)
has a Soul somewhere inside him or her,
and that the Soul lives on forever,
even after the body dies.

Now, no one has ever seen a Soul,
so we can't even be sure
that there really is such a thing.
But if you believe
that everyone does have a Soul,
then what happens to the Soul
after a person dies?

To find out,
maybe we can start by reading books
to learn what different religions
and cultures believe happens to the Soul
after Death.

We can also talk to the leaders and teachers
of different religions and cultures
to find out what they believe
happens to the Soul after Death.

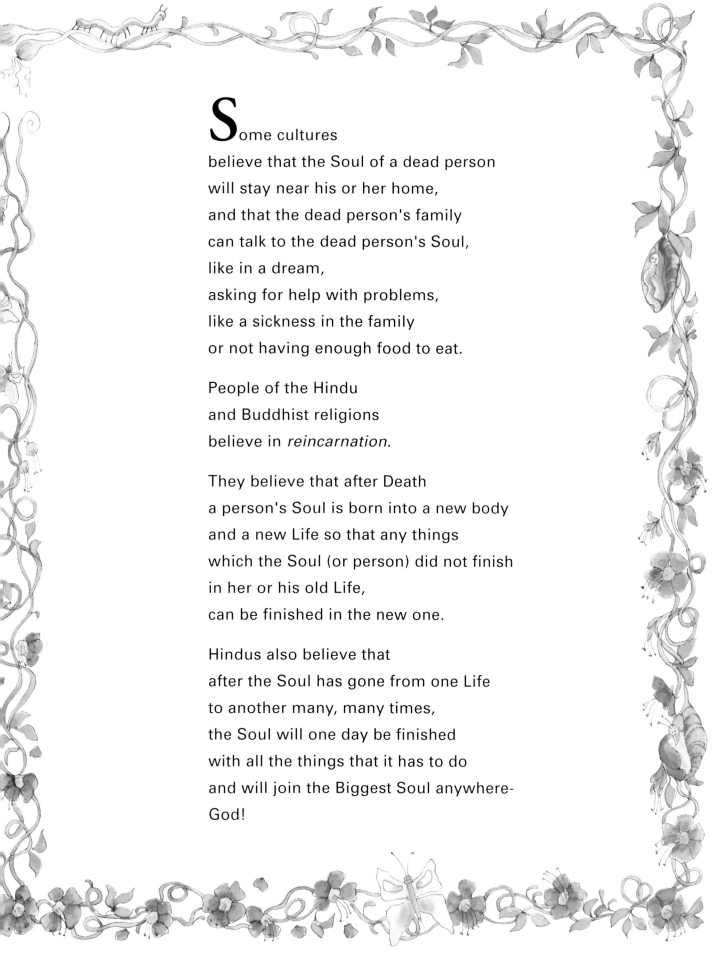

Some cultures
believe that the Soul of a dead person
will stay near his or her home,
and that the dead person's family
can talk to the dead person's Soul,
like in a dream,
asking for help with problems,
like a sickness in the family
or not having enough food to eat.

People of the Hindu
and Buddhist religions
believe in *reincarnation*.

They believe that after Death
a person's Soul is born into a new body
and a new Life so that any things
which the Soul (or person) did not finish
in her or his old Life,
can be finished in the new one.

Hindus also believe that
after the Soul has gone from one Life
to another many, many times,
the Soul will one day be finished
with all the things that it has to do
and will join the Biggest Soul anywhere-
God!

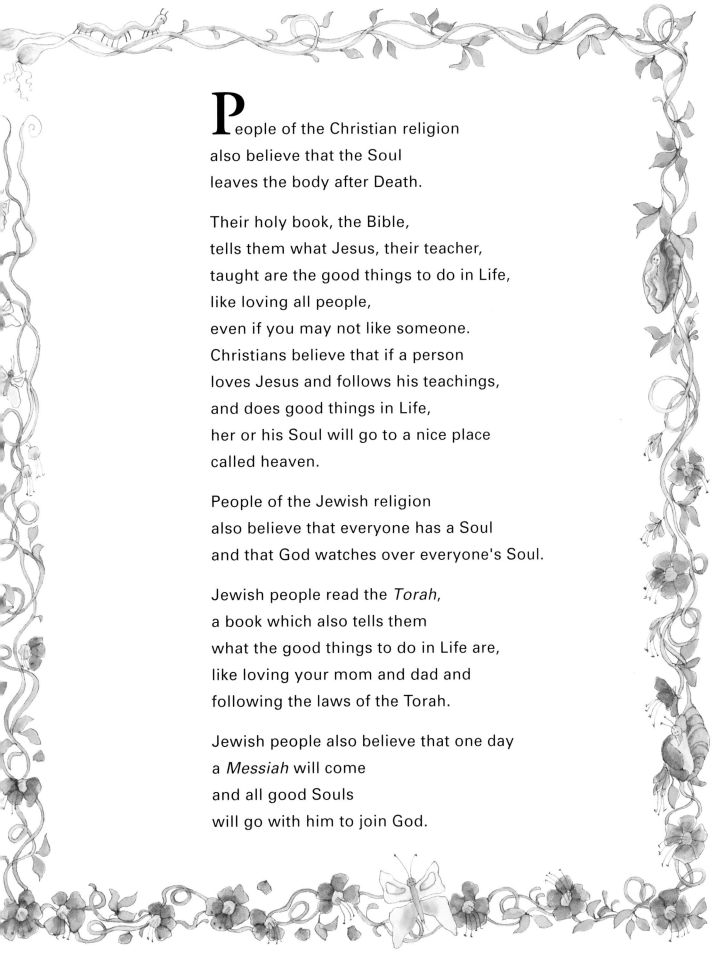

People of the Christian religion
also believe that the Soul
leaves the body after Death.

Their holy book, the Bible,
tells them what Jesus, their teacher,
taught are the good things to do in Life,
like loving all people,
even if you may not like someone.
Christians believe that if a person
loves Jesus and follows his teachings,
and does good things in Life,
her or his Soul will go to a nice place
called heaven.

People of the Jewish religion
also believe that everyone has a Soul
and that God watches over everyone's Soul.

Jewish people read the *Torah*,
a book which also tells them
what the good things to do in Life are,
like loving your mom and dad and
following the laws of the Torah.

Jewish people also believe that one day
a *Messiah* will come
and all good Souls
will go with him to join God.

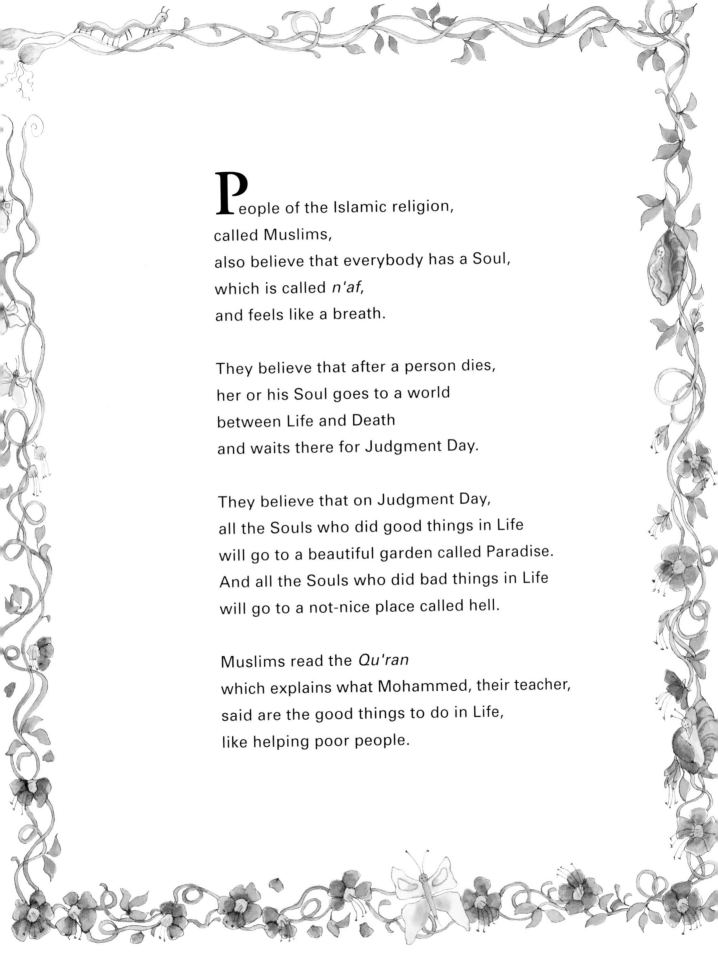

People of the Islamic religion,
called Muslims,
also believe that everybody has a Soul,
which is called *n'af*,
and feels like a breath.

They believe that after a person dies,
her or his Soul goes to a world
between Life and Death
and waits there for Judgment Day.

They believe that on Judgment Day,
all the Souls who did good things in Life
will go to a beautiful garden called Paradise.
And all the Souls who did bad things in Life
will go to a not-nice place called hell.

Muslims read the *Qu'ran*
which explains what Mohammed, their teacher,
said are the good things to do in Life,
like helping poor people.

So, even though we know
what people of different cultures
and religions believe about Death
and what happens to the Soul after Death,
there are also many people
who do *not* believe
that each person has a Soul
or that anything happens to a person
after he or she dies.

There are people who believe
that nothing happens after we die,
that Death is like a door we go through
which closes behind us forever.

We can't really say
that these people are wrong,
or that only one religion
or one culture is right
about the mystery of Death.

Most of the great teachers,
like Jesus and Buddha,
never really talked about Death,
maybe because they did not want
people to think more about Death
than about doing good things in Life.

Maybe these great teachers
did not feel that What is Death?
is such a big question
because they knew that we really die
and are born every day.

How can we die
and be born every day?

When we go to sleep at night
and wake up in the morning,
we are still the same person
but it is a new day
and it's almost like
being born again.

When we go on a trip
to a strange new place,
we are still the same person,
but it's like being born again
in a new and different place.

When we learn an important lesson
in Life,
we let an old part of us die
and a new part be born.

Maybe Death is really like that.

Maybe Death is not a sad or scary thing.
Maybe Death is like moving
from one thing to another,
from an old home to a new home,
or like going from one land
to another land,
only a little further away.

Maybe we can do something
so that we can live on forever,
even after Death!

How can we live on forever
even after Death?
Maybe by doing something really, really nice
for somebody, or for a lot of people,
where we even have to make a sacrifice.
(To sacrifice means to give something of ours away
that is really hard for us to give away.)

Maybe by making a sacrifice,
we or our Souls can live on forever
in other people's hearts,
where they remember us in a good way,
even after we die!

So, maybe Death is not like
closing a door
and never being able to open it again.
Maybe Death is only a place
where a person,
and his or her Soul,
live on forever
in other people's hearts.

Like your friend's Grandpa,
whom your friend always remembers
and loves
because his Grandpa gave him so much love.
Maybe your friend feels, in some ways,
that his Grandpa never really died!

So, maybe if we start to think of Death
in all these good ways,
we'll be able to do good
and loving things in Life.
And, by doing good and loving things
in Life, maybe we can start
to answer that big question
What is Death?